THE ENGLISH CIVIL WAR

A Living History

THE ENGLISH CIVIL WAR

A Living History

PAUL LEWIS ISEMONGER

ALAN SUTTON PUBLISHING LIMITED

First published in the United Kingdom in 1994
Alan Sutton Publishing Ltd · Phoenix Mill · Far Thrupp · Stroud
Gloucestershire

Reprinted, with corrections, 1995

British Library Cataloguing-in-Publication Data

Isemonger, Paul Lewis
  The English Civil War: A Living History
  I. Title
  942.062

  ISBN 0-7509-0555-7

Typeset in 11/14 Baskerville.
Typesetting and origination by
Alan Sutton Publishing Limited.
Printed in Great Britain by
WBC Ltd, Bridgend.

CONTENTS

FOREWORD

Interest in our English Civil War has never been greater than it is today – an interest based on the realization that it was indeed a momentous period in the history of our island and one from which our present parliamentary system has evolved.

Although the basic facts of the Civil War have long been known, there has, until recently, been little interest shown in the detail – how the weapons were constructed and loaded, what the drills were, how the tactics in the field developed, how the armies were garrisoned, clothed and fed.

With the emergence of the Sealed Knot and the English Civil War Society, all this has changed.

The late Brigadier Peter Young DSO MC, legendary commando leader in the last war and distinguished military historian, founded the Sealed Knot and fired all those who joined with his enthusiasm.

Above all he stressed the obligation to research the detail, to be authentic and to aim for total realism.

Those who have not participated or who do not even know of the activities of the two societies may, after reading this book, ask the question 'How do I become a member?' They will find a list of addresses within this book; good luck to them and to all who appear in the photographs, and warm congratulations to the author for assembling such important historical material.

The Rt. Hon. The Lord Saye and Sele,
Broughton Castle, Oxfordshire,
May 1994

Historical note:

THE 8TH LORD SAYE AND SELE AND THE CIVIL WAR

William Fiennes 8th Lord Saye and Sele was involved in the political life of the country during forty crucial years in the seventeenth century. He supported James I, who stayed at Broughton and made William a viscount.

However, as a liberal-minded man, he was opposed to Charles I's autocratic rule without parliament and became one of the leaders of those who sought to control the activities of the King.

Refusing to take the oath of allegiance or to pay Ship Money – a tax imposed by the King – Charles expressed his disapproval saying to William 'I find you averse to all my proceedings'.

At the start of the Civil War, William raised his regiment of Bluecoats to fight on the side of Parliament against the King. Broughton was surrendered to the Royalists after the Battle of Edgehill in 1642.

William was nothing if not consistent and came to oppose Cromwell's autocratic rule and his execution of the King as thoroughly as he had opposed the King in earlier times. At the restoration of Charles II in 1660 William was pardoned and took his place on the King's Privy Council.

William had earned the name 'Old Subtlety' from those that disapproved of him and certainly he must have seemed devious to some. Clarendon, the Royalist historian, said of him: 'He had a hand in all the evils that befell the unhappy Kingdom'. His influence and significance has certainly been underated; above all he was a man of liberal convictions.

After all the tribulations, dangers and confusions of the seventeenth century William died in his bed in 1662 aged eighty.

ACKNOWLEDGEMENTS

I am indebted to the following people for their help in the preparation of this book: Paul Meekins, for his enthusiasm and willingness to share his expertise; Ian Barrett and the Fairfax Battalia ECWS, for their generous help; Alan Turton at Basing House for proof-reading; John Litchfield and Colonel George Monck's Regiment of Foote, for their authentic musket drill, and for laying down in freezing cold mud for the 'death' scenes; Mr Jeffrey Parker and Winchesters Regiment ECWS for the sutlers, and for the 'Col. Windibanke' sequence at Stokesay Castle; the Two J's for supplying authentic pole-arms, muskets, swords and leatherwork; Graham and Max of the SK for repeatedly charging their horses across a field for some of the action shots (with Graham in full curassier armour); Geoff Baker of ECWS for supplying some of the firearms; Partizan Press, 818 London Road, Leigh-on-Sea, Essex, for allowing me to quote from *The Edgehill Campaign and the Letters of Nehemiah Wharton* (page 9) and Richard Symonds, *The Complete Military Diary* (pages 135–8). I would like to acknowledge the valuable research material contained within *Civil War Notes and Queries* (Partizan Press), and Roger Emmerson of Captayne Henry Hazzards Company of Firelockes and Artillerie, ECWS.

A number of the photographs were taken at English Heritage properties. I would like to thank Howard Giles, the Head of Special Events, for the opportunity to photograph these authentic displays. The atmospheric and dramatic English Heritage properties are a perfect back-drop for photography.

My special thanks go to all the re-enactors – too many to name individually – whose enthusiasm and unfailing good humour, in often cold and difficult circumstances, have made this book possible.

Finally my very special thanks to Joan and Marilyn for supplying twentieth-century practicalities while I was living in the seventeenth century.

Paul Lewis Isemonger

PICTURE CREDITS

INTRODUCTION

Since the invention of a portable photographic system in the
nineteenth century, the world has not been allowed to escape the
brutal realism of warfare. Photographers, often risking their own
lives, have brought startling and disturbing images to our breakfast tables.
From the corpse-strewn fields of Gettysburg of 1863, to the joy and relief
of the liberated French in the Second World War. From the haunting
image of a slaughtered native American chief at Wounded Knee in 1891
to the strutting megalomania of European warlords.

Whole libraries are full of images of more recent conflicts, putting a
human face to the heroism and hell of war, but how do we perceive pre-
nineteenth-century struggles? What is known about the everyday life of
soldiers in the Battle of Hastings; Agincourt; the English Civil War? The
truth is that a great deal of accurate information is known, but in the
absence of photographic evidence it is the colourful inaccuracies that
persist. Some of these, no doubt, sprang from Victorian romanticism
and, later, were enthusiastically encouraged by countless swashbuckling
movies.

The few images that do come down to us from the English Civil War,
arguably one of the most important eras of British history, tend to be the
rather dry and stiff portraits depicting leaders as they wished to be
recorded. The aim of this book is to bring the English Civil War out from
behind the yellowing varnish of dusty paintings and into today's world of
the photographic image.

In Great Britain today we are lucky to have several dedicated English
Civil War groups. In the production of this book I have been able to
draw on the wealth of knowledge and authentic re-enactment that exists
among the ranks of The English Civil War Society (ECWS) and the
Sealed Knot (SK).

Many of the images that you will see in the following pages are the
results of years of research and a determination by their members to find
out how a seventeenth-century soldier actually lived and fought during a
bloody civil conflict. Within their ranks are people specializing in different
aspects of seventeenth-century life, from military drill and procedure, to

the types of food available to soldiers and civilians; from enthusiasts of seventeenth-century dialects, to craftspeople producing accurate facsimiles of weapons and armour. All this and more contribute to a living history that continually has to adjust in the light of new knowledge.

CHRONOLOGY

THE ROAD TO CIVIL WAR

The relationship between the autocratic King Charles I and Parliament had been uneasy for some years and was now being aggravated by the imposition of taxes and the King's apparent leanings towards the Catholic Church.

The King sought to rule without Parliament, but in 1639 and 1640 the Scots Wars forced the King to summon Parliament once again. Parliament now sought the removal of the King's advisers and tighter control over the powers of the Crown.

After protracted disagreements the King left London and on 22 August 1642 the Royal Standard was raised in Nottingham. The King and Parliament were at war.

1642

The first major clash between the two armies happens at Edgehill on 23 October, the outcome does not favour either side.

The King fails to march on London and occupies Oxford as his headquarters.

1643

Much of the north is occupied by Royalist forces under the Earl of Newcastle.

Sir Ralph Hopton's Cornish army, fighting for the Royalist cause, has a string of military successes in the south-west, but fails to take Plymouth.

Prince Rupert, the King's nephew, captures Bristol, but fails to take Gloucester which is relieved by the army of the Earl of Essex in September. The King's army is forced to withdraw after fighting for twelve hours at the first Battle of Newbury on 20 September.

A Scottish force is sent to aid Parliament in the north-east.

Despite numerous successes in gaining territory, the Royalists end the year without a major victory.

1644

On 25 January the King is defeated at Nantwich despite the recent addition of troops brought back from Ireland.

On 2 July the largest battle of the war ends on Marston Moor with the massive defeat of Prince Rupert.

The King's Oxford army has increasing success in the south and south-west.

Scotland sees a Royalist rebellion headed by the Marquis of Montrose.

1645

Parliament forms the New Model Army, led by Sir Thomas Fairfax and Oliver Cromwell.

On 14 June the Oxford army of the King is overwhelmed and defeated at Naseby by the efficient New Model Army.

On 10 July the New Model Army continues its success and defeats the Royalist Western Army at Langport.

Fairfax and Cromwell start eliminating the Royalist garrisons.

Although briefly successful, the Royalist rebellion fails at Philliphaugh in Scotland.

1646

The remnants of the King's field armies surrender, marking the end of the first Civil War.

The King seeks refuge in Scotland.

The last of the major Royalist garrisons fall.

1648

A series of Royalist uprisings in England and Wales marks the beginning of the second Civil War.

The Duke of Hamilton leads a Scottish army into England in support of the King, where they are defeated by Cromwell.

The remaining English Royalists are defeated by Fairfax at Colchester.

1649

Following the execution of King Charles I, the monarchy is abolished in England and Wales.

The Commonwealth is established.

The suppression of the Irish rebellion is begun by Cromwell.

1650

Charles II prepares to invade England with the support of the Scots.

On 3 September the Scots, under David Lesley, are defeated at Dunbar by Cromwell.

1651

Charles II invades England but receives little English support.

Having abandoned his march to London, Charles sets up a base at Worcester.

In the Battle of Worcester (3 September) Cromwell's army defeats Charles II who flees the country.

The wars are over and Cromwell remains as Lord Protector until he dies in 1658.

Charles II is returned to the throne in 1660.

Parliamentarians and Royalists

During the years leading up to the war, the army was seriously under strength. This was exemplified by the King's inability to repulse the Scottish army when they occupied Northumberland and Durham during the Scots Wars. However, the King did possess a unit of well-trained cavalry under the command of Lord Holland, which formed part of a relatively small national army. The pre-war infantry units were called the Trained Bands, made up of mostly middle-class property owners or their sons. The London Trained Bands were to prove very important to the Parliamentary armies of Essex and Waller.

At the outset of war the only sizeable military force in England was the artillery, known as the Board of Ordinance and based at the Tower of London.

The main field armies were divided into three principal groups: the infantry, which was composed of musketeers and pikemen; the great horse and dragoons of the cavalry; and the artillery.

The INFANTRY

The pikemen.

A musketeer.

The officers. Many officers were experienced soldiers, having served in Germany during the Thirty Years' War.

Each infantry company had its own flag or colour carried by an ensign.

The drummer was essential in order to transmit orders during the noise and confusion of the battlefield.

The supplies were carried by the baggage train, which was divided into 'official' and 'unofficial'. The official baggage comprised shot, powder and match for the artillery and musketeers; tools and spare parts; food; plus a number of civilians attached to the unit such as chaplains, clerks and cooks (known as sutlers). The unofficial baggage was made up of the private possessions of officers and cavalry troopers plus their servants.

The CAVALRY

The great horse formed the main attack force of an army.

Dragoons were mounted infantry, only rarely fighting on horseback.

The ARTILLERY

A wide range of artillery weapons were available, from large siege pieces able to knock holes in castle walls, to smaller anti-personnel guns.

A solid iron cannon-ball would have a devastating effect on infantry, ricocheting through the closely formed ranks and causing horrific injuries.

The Armies at War

'With about three thousand foot and four hundred horse, we came to Southam . . . This is a very malignant towne . . . We pillaged the minister, and took from him a drum and severall armes . . . our soldiers, wearied out, quartered themselves about the towne . . . an alarum cryed "arme, arme, for the enemy is commenge," . . . all our soildiers were cannybals in armes . . . crynge out for a dish of Calvellaers to supper . . . our enemise intended to set upon us before wee could gather our companies together . . . Being on fier to be at them wee marched thorow the corne and got the hill of them, whereupon they played upon us their ordinances, but they came short . . . After we gave them eight shot more, whereupon all their foote companies fled and offered their armes in the towns adjacent for twelve pence a peece. Ther troops, whelinge about, toke up their dead bodies and fled . . .'

The CAVALRY

The outcome of a battle was often determined by the actions of the cavalry, which formed troops under the authority of a captain.

Troops usually consisted of about sixty troopers plus officers and non-commissioned officers (NCOs). They were formed into groups of five or six troops to form a regiment under the command of a colonel.

The cavalry was formed into the great horse and the dragoons.

Dragoons.

The great horse consisted largely of troopers known as harquebusiers.

Troopers purchased their own clothes, although armour would usually have been supplied by the regiment.

A harquebusier wearing a helmet known as a 'pott'. This example has three vertical face protectors attached to a hinged peak, and is typical of the English style of construction. The crown could either be formed from a single piece of metal or from two separate halves, with the seam running from front to back. The back of the neck was protected by a single metal plate.

An accurate reproduction of a zischarge helmet, with a set of articulated metal plates to protect the neck. The original is likely to have come from Germany. This style of helmet had a single sliding nasal bar and a fixed peak.

The harquebusier wore a thick hide coat, extending to the thigh and covering the arms, known as a buff coat. If the trooper could afford a good quality example he might dispense with the heavy and uncomfortable back and breast plates. The average cost of a buff coat was 30 shillings.

A dismounted harquebusier wearing a montero hat and carrying his helmet and fire-lock pistol. The origins of the harquebusier date back to previous centuries when he was a foot soldier armed with a crossbow. Around the end of the fifteenth century the crossbow was exchanged for a primitive gun called a harquebus. The next development was to mount the harquebusier on horseback as the French did in their wars against the Italians. Eventually the harquebusier became the cavalryman typical of the armies of western Europe during the seventeenth century.

An example of an elbow gauntlet (reproduction), sometimes worn by the harquebusier to protect his bridle arm. They seem to have fallen out of use during the war. Some examples made from buff leather are known.

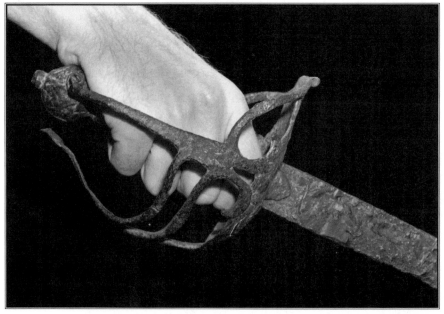

An original mortuary-hilted, single-edged sword, a type favoured by the cavalry. This rather corroded example was found in the thatch of an old cidermill house near Gloucester in 1926. Although the blade has lost the very tip, it still retains a relatively sharp edge. The cutting edge of the blade near the hilt has numerous dents, indicating probable combat use. This was the strongest part of the blade and was used to parry an opponent's blows.

One of the finest collections of Civil War arms and armour was bought for the nation by the Royal Armouries, and is housed at Littlecote near Hungerford.

During the seventeenth century Littlecote belonged to the Popham family. Colonels Edward and Alexander Popham fought for Parliament during the Civil War. The house was garrisoned for Parliament.

During the early part of the war there was considerable variation in the styles of equipment and clothes among individual troopers.

The main battle tactics of the cavalry were going through a state of change at this time. In previous years the cavalry had been armed with lances and their main assault tactic was the charge at full gallop. Following the invention of firearms a new system had been evolved on the continent. The German Reiters were foremost in the use of long pistols. Line after line of cavalrymen would ride at a trot towards the lines of infantry and discharge their weapons until a path had been cleared through them. The Swedish King, Gustavus Adolphus, had brought innovations to cavalry tactics that were to have a lasting effect on English cavalry. He advised that the charge should be at a more rapid pace, and always to charge home, while reserving their pistol fire until the enemy had fired first. There was a brief struggle at the beginning of the Civil War between proponents of both tactics, but the Swedish method was adopted first by the Royalists and later by the Parliamentarians.

The task for the cavalry was to engage and overwhelm the opposing cavalry. This having been achieved they would harry the foot soldiers.

The colours carried by each troop of horse or company of dragoons were called cornets. They were smaller than the colours carried by the infantry. Cornets were highly prized battle trophies and ferociously protected.

Open fields were the favoured fighting ground for the great horse, but rabbit warrens or sudden undulations could, and often did, break up a charge before it could engage the enemy.

If the cavalry trooper of the great horse was well equipped, which was not always the case, a pair of high 'bucket top' boots were worn.

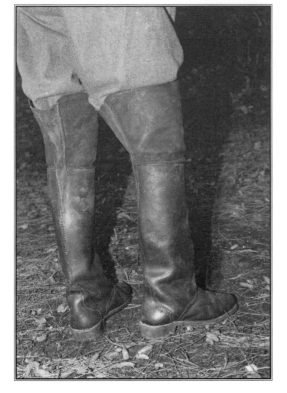

Bucket tops in the extended position for riding. This pair has been adapted by the insertion of a piece of leather to widen the top.

During the latter stages of the war the cavalry often made up 50 per cent of the forces deployed. This was particularly so with the Royalist army.

The horses suffered greatly; the troopers used vicious spurs, and the inaccurate musket ball was more likely to hit the relatively large target of the horse than the man.

Messages carried by troopers were essential in keeping open the lines of communication. The storming of Cirencester in Gloucestershire in 1643 was an important victory for the Royalists. It kept open a line of communication between Oxford, the King's headquarters, and the west.

Each cavalry troop had two trumpeters, who were vital for signalling the commands of the captain. They often had more elaborate uniforms than their fellow soldiers, paid for by the captain. A trumpeter would also act as a messenger. Hanging from the valveless trumpet was a banner, usually the personal coat of arms of the captain.

The Royalist and Parliamentarian armies were virtually indistinguishable. This obvious disadvantage to both sides led to the adoption of field signs such as a sprig of oak leaves or, more frequently, different coloured sashes. The Royalists wore red and the Parliamentarians orange tawny.

The cavalry was generally made up of gentlemen and their servants, or small farmers.

A relatively small proportion of the great horse was made up of the curassiers, who were equipped with armour that stretched from head to knee. This heavy steel armour could resist the passage of a pistol ball. With the addition of a piece of armour called a placket, some areas were musket proof.

The armour of a curassier was very heavy and uncomfortable to wear. Heatstroke and dehydration during a battle that could last all day must have been a major problem in the heat of summer. One of the few units of curassiers to be raised during the course of the war was that of Sir Arthur Hazelrigg. Known as Hazelrigg's Lobsters, they were defeated at the battle of Roundway Down in 1643. They were routed and pursued over a steep slope, where many men and horses were killed and injured. By the end of the war use of heavily armoured curassiers had ceased.

Skilfully constructed overlapping metal plates ensured a reasonable amount of movement for the mounted curassier.

Curassiers frequently formed the General Officers Lifeguard.

The horses required to support a man in heavy armour were scarce in England during the
Civil War.

Both the harquebusiers and curassiers were equipped with firearms, usually consisting of
two pistols and/or a carbine (a short-barrelled musket). The mechanism used to fire the
weapon was unlikely to be the basic matchlock, which would have been difficult to use on
horseback. The favoured firearm was either the wheel-lock or the flintlock. The illustrated
example is a reproduction of a wheel-lock. The principle of the wheel-lock was discovered
in the sixteenth century. A small piece of iron pyrites was held against a serrated iron wheel
which was made to rotate rapidly against it. This produced a shower of sparks which fell
into the pan and ignited the priming powder. Many of the wheel-lock weapons used during
the Civil War were of Dutch origin.

The internal mechanism of a wheel-lock. These weapons were more expensive to produce than the flintlock. If the mechanism of a wheel-lock was left wound up for any length of time, even overnight, there was a strong probability that it would not fire.

A reproduction firelock pistol, with an external catch to hold back the cock. This type of lock was called a dog-lock.

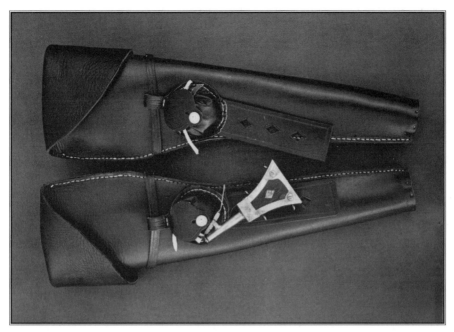

The cavalry kept their pistols strapped one either side of the horse in leather holsters. These highly accurate reproductions show the small pouches for the lead shot and a flask for the black powder.

An alternative weapon for the cavalry was the pole-axe, an effective weapon against an armoured opponent.

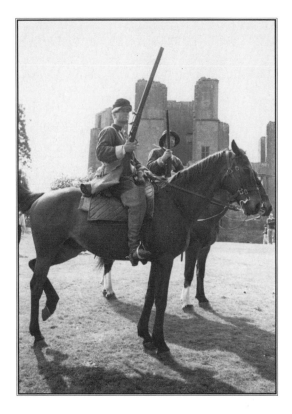

Dragoons were the second main force of the cavalry. Generally these mounted infantrymen were equipped with firelock muskets, although because of a lack of funds the Kings Dragoons were often armed with matchlocks. Dragoons rode to the battle or skirmish, dismounted and fought on foot, one in ten of the men stayed behind the battle line to hold the horses. However, there are a few recorded incidents of dragoons delivering mounted attacks in the style of the great horse. At the outset of war complete regiments of dragoons were formed, but during the course of the war they tended to form single troops attached to regiments of horse.

Dragoons were looked upon as a cheap form of cavalry, often riding inferior quality horses, but in fact they were an efficient fighting force able to deliver firepower when it was needed quickly. Their main role was to defend the great horse in exposed positions and defend lines of communication. They were also involved in scouting, raiding and skirmishing. Shoes were favoured by dragoons, cumbersome boots would have slowed down a man fighting on foot. The shot and powder was carried in a bandolier across the shoulder or in a leather box or bag around the waist. The clothes worn were what the soldier could afford. The soldier in the photograph is wearing a short leather jerkin.

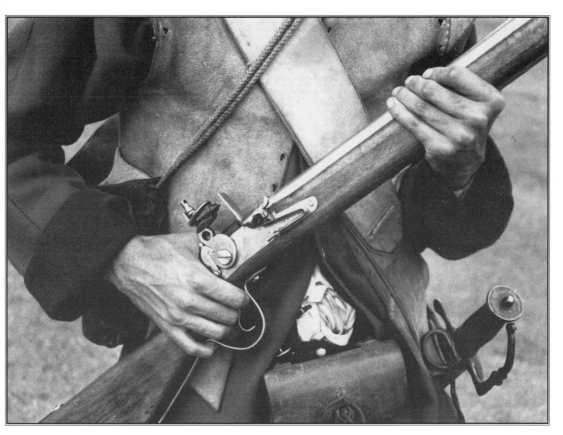

The firelock musket was the 'state of the art' weapon. The lock was more prone to mechanical failure than the matchlock, but overall was more reliable, particularly in wet weather when keeping a length of match burning was extremely difficult. When the trigger was pulled it released a pre-tensioned clamp called a cock. The jaws of the cock contained a piece of flint which struck a vertical metal bar known as the frizzen. The contact between flint and frizzen sent a shower of sparks into the pan igniting the powder and, via a touch-hole, the main charge.

The INFANTRY

The infantry, comprising musketeers and pikemen, were formed into companies which in turn would make up regiments.

An average regiment of pikemen and musketeers would contain 250–300 men. Each company had its own flag, known as a colour.

In practice, companies did not fight as individual units but formed into two basic fighting structures: firstly, a pike battaile of 150–200 pikemen flanked on either side by 50 musketeers, and secondly, a musket block of 48 men commanded by a lieutenant and a sergeant. A typical formation would have been six deep.

During the early stages of the war soldiers often wore their civilian clothes.

Two musketeers to one pikeman would have been the typical ratio, although this could vary considerably.

Volunteers were plentiful at the start of the war. Many of them were apprentices, ranging in age from thirteen to twenty-one. Officially, military age was sixteen to sixty.

Other volunteers were agricultural workers
(right), craftsmen such as carpenters and
woodturners (above left) or shoe makers
(above right).

As the war progressed, volunteers were not so easy to find. Parish Constables were given the task of supplying conscripted men for the army. They were taken from among the unemployed, criminals from local gaols, and vagabonds. This lack of committed fighting men often led to desertion just before or during battles.

A high proportion of the casualties occurred after they had been routed.

Many battles and skirmishes were fought in close country.

Firing from behind the shelter of trees and hedges was a common tactic.

Large field battles were the exception rather than the rule. An army undertaking this form of combat would present a maximum of 12,000 men to face the enemy.

The line of battle could stretch up to 2 miles across.

A typical field battle would begin with a bombardment by the artillery.

Then, a 'Forlorn Hope' of musketeers would engage the enemy's regiments of foot soldiers. The term 'Forlorn Hope' came from the Dutch *Verloren Hoop* or 'Lost Troop'. They were a body of men chosen to attack the enemy ahead of the main army. The casualty rate of such a group was very high.

The cavalry would be waiting on both flanks, and when certain that the enemy were showing signs of weakening they would charge. The intention was to destroy the opposing cavalry.

A ferocious sword and pistol battle would ensue.

During the Battle of Edgehill, Prince Rupert's cavalry mistakenly thought that the day had been won and rode off the field in search of the enemy's baggage train.

It would take some time to reform the victorious cavalry.

A battaile of pike and musket. While the cavalry were fighting the infantry would push forward.

It is not difficult to imagine the sort of injury a sharp pike point could inflict when aimed at the head, throat or any other unprotected part of the body.

Pikemen had to be fit and strong to wield the heavy and awkward pike, particularly when the wind was blowing.

Pike blocks fighting 'at point'.

Initial casualties were relatively few when pike blocks met.

It was not until one side gained an advantage, possibly aided by the cavalry or the steady pressure from the musketeers, that casualties in any number occurred.

Pressing home the advantage with drawn swords.

Once a side had the upper hand, a rout with heavy casualties was likely. The fleeing infantry were also likely to be run down by the cavalry.

Meanwhile the musketeers were firing steadily. Each musketeer could fire about twice every minute.

One form of attack used by musketeers was to present a single or double file of soldiers to fire at the enemy, while keeping the main body of musketeers in the shelter of trees or hills.

When the file of musketeers had fired, they would retire to the sheltered position and be replaced with the next file.

Although musketeers were supplied with swords, the favoured weapon for hand to hand fighting was the musket used as a club.

The pikemen were very effective at keeping the cavalry at bay.

Horses would not charge a wall of bristling pikes. Without the support of their infantry the cavalry would find a pike block virtually impenetrable.

If a cavalry trooper was unfortunate enough to become embroiled with the pike his chances were not good.

The victorious side would loot the camp and baggage train of the losers.

The dead were stripped of valuable shoes, clothes, arms and armour.

Generally speaking, captured
foot soldiers were well treated.
Most officers were exchanged
although some were shot. It was
a common occurrence for a foot
soldier to re-enlist with his
captors.

Mutiny, particularly at small
garrisons, was often caused by
low pay or an over-zealous and
unpopular officer.

Theoretically, the musketeer could be effective at 400 paces using his smooth bore matchlock musket. Realistically the useful range was 50 yards.

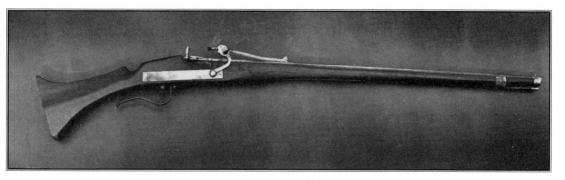

The basic matchlock musket measured 42 to 48 inches.

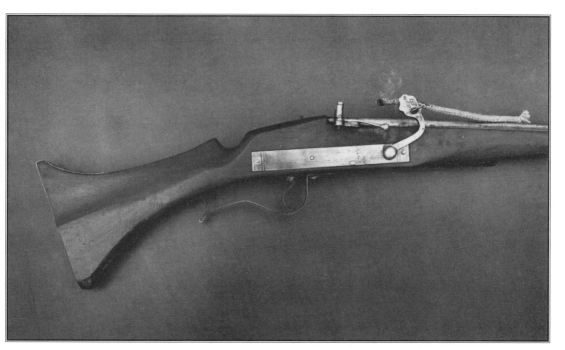

A smouldering length of rope soaked in saltpetre was used to ignite the priming powder. The match was clamped into the 'serpent'. When the trigger was pulled the serpent lowered the match into the priming pan. Gunpowder was a mixture of sulphur, charcoal and saltpetre.

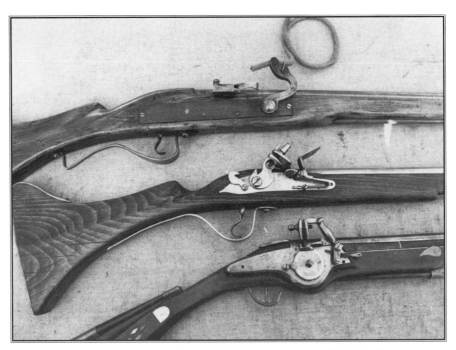

A comparison of the three firing mechanisms available during the Civil War (from top to bottom): matchlock, firelock (flintlock), wheel-lock.

The internal mechanism of the matchlock. Because of its simplicity of design, the matchlock was favoured for mass production rather than the more modern firelock.

Each musketeer was issued with a bandolier of small wooden or tin containers. Each container held sufficient gunpowder for one shot. The bandolier was worn across the body from left shoulder to right hip. This method of storing powder speeded up reloading.

When conflict was imminent, the match was kept burning constantly. Because of the danger of carrying a glowing match with the bandolier full of gunpowder, the match was detached from the musket and held in the left hand. Both ends were kept alight and held between the fingers. Musketeers refilled their bandolier from the unit's powder barrel known as the 'budge barrel'. There were several recorded events of the hasty musketeer plunging his hand containing the match into the budge barrel with disastrous consequences.

The bandolier also contained a small leather bag for shot, a powder flask for the fine priming powder, and a thin metal spike called a pricker for keeping the touch-hole clean. The bandolier would hold twelve to fifteen containers.

A highly accurate representation of a Civil War musketeer. The pay for musketeers was 8d. a day, or less if he was in a garrison.

This musketeer is wearing a snapsack across his back. This would have been made from canvas or leather, and was for personal possessions. The knitted woollen cap was called a monmouth.

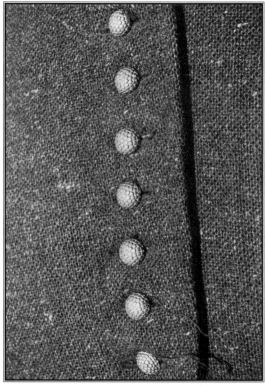

Some replica seventeenth-century buttons.

An alternative form of headwear was the montero. Styled on the Spanish hunting cap, this warm and comfortable hat was made from wool. It could be worn rolled up (right) or pulled down like a balaclava (below).

At the start of the war, rests were used to support the cumbersome muskets. These were found to be impractical as the war progressed and were dispensed with.

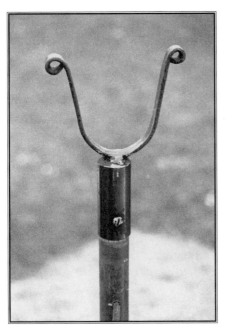

A reproduction of a musket rest.

Swords, issued by the army, were of inferior quality. Each musketeer carried a sword, but they were more useful for chopping firewood than fighting.

A pair of well used 'latchet hole' shoes. Each shoe could be worn on either foot. This enabled the wearer to swap shoes over to even out the wear on the sole.

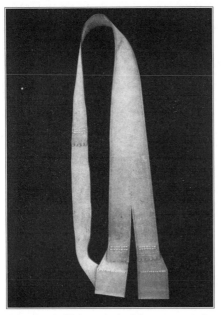

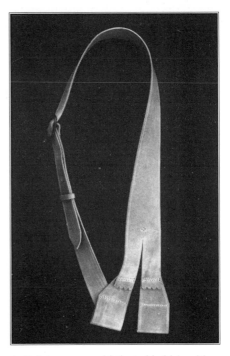

A leather baldric typical of the sort worn by musketeers. The sword was held in place by the two lower loops. The baldric was worn across the body from right shoulder to left hip. This example is an exact copy of an original in the Tower Armouries collection at Littlecote.

A slightly more sophisticated baldric with a buckle.

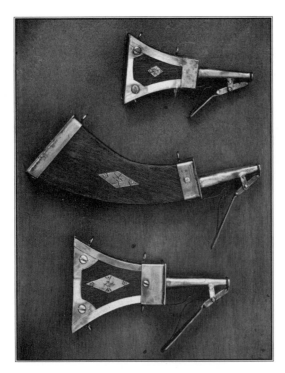

Powder flasks made from steel and wood.

Musket balls, hand-cast from lead, weighed about 1¹/₄ ounces.

A stock of newly cast musket balls.

THE LOADING AND FIRING OF A MATCHLOCK MUSKET

Loading and firing a matchlock musket was potentially dangerous for the musketeer, requiring a lighted length of match to be handled at the same time as using gunpowder. A strict discipline was necessary to reduce the risk of self inflicted injury. The following musket drill is typical of that found in seventeenth-century drill books. The captions are the words that would have been spoken by the NCO when training the musketeers. Although this process might seem overly complex, a trained musketeer could fire up to twice per minute.

1. Give rest to your musket.

2. Open your pan.

7. Blow off your loose powder.

8. Cast about your musket.

13. Reverse and shorten your scouring stick.

14. Ram home.

19. Draw forth your match.

20. Blow your cole.

3. Clear your pan.

4. Prime your pan.

5. Shut your pan.

6. Cast off your loose powder.

9. Open your charge.

10. Charge with powder.

11. Charge with bullet.

12. Draw forth your scouring stick.

15. Withdraw your scouring stick.

16. Reverse and shorten your scouring stick.

17. Return your scouring stick.

18. Give rest to your musket.

21. Cock your match.

22. Guard and blow.

23. Open your pan.

24. Present and give fire.

1. The priming pan cover is swung open.

2. Any debris is blown out of the pan.

5. Any loose grains of powder are removed by first turning the musket over . . .

6. . . . and then by blowing across the top of the closed pan.

9. A musket ball is taken out of the small leather bag on the bandolier.

10. The ball is placed in the barrel followed by a wad of either paper or dried vegetation.

3. The priming powder is put into the pan.

4. The priming pan is closed.

7. One of the boxes of powder hanging from the bandolier is opened.

8. The pre-measured powder is tipped into the muzzle of the barrel.

11. The scouring stick (in later centuries called a ramrod) is withdrawn from beneath the barrel.

12. The scouring stick is placed in the muzzle.

13. The charge is rammed home.

14. The ash is removed from the slow-burning match.

15. The match is placed in the cock. Great care is taken to ensure that the match is positioned exactly above the pan.

16. The priming pan is covered by the right hand and the match is blown once more.

17. The priming pan is opened and the musket is aimed.

18. The trigger is pulled and the match descends into the priming pan. The powder ignites and, via a touch-hole, the main charge is fired.

The pike was a sixteen foot ash pole tipped with a metal point. In practice, the pike was often a few feet less, having been shortened to provide fuel for winter fires. The shorter length also made the pike easier to handle.

The well-equipped pikeman was issued with back and breast armour, sometimes supplemented with thigh armour known as tassets. The pike was regarded as the honourable weapon.

Pikemen were more likely to use their swords in battle than the musketeers.

Although armour was ideal for pikemen, the cost of equipping a whole regiment was high, and many regiments of pike fought without any armour.

The pay for pikemen was the same as musketeers at 8d. a day. This was roughly the equivalent of an agricultural worker's pay.

A favoured type of helmet was the morion. This design had remained almost unchanged since the sixteenth century.

An alternative design for a pikeman's pott. This example is a copy of an original found in the Royal Armouries reserve collection.

Like the musketeers, the pikemen formed an efficient fighting force because of their ability
to adhere to a rigid drill.

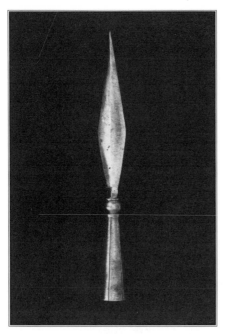

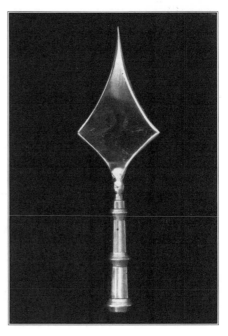

An accurate facsimile of a pike point in the Tower Armouries collection.

An alternative design for a pike point. The original is in the Amsterdam Historisches Museum.

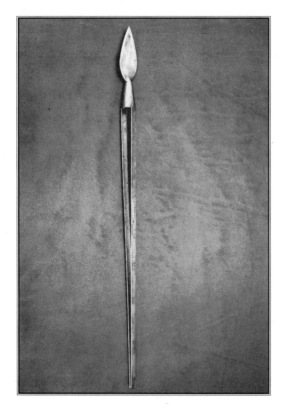

A third design showing the langets. These metal strips extended two feet down the pike, and prevented the tip from being hacked off.

Position for marching (the order given, 'Shoulder your pike').

Ready for action (the order given, 'Charge your pike').

Charge your pike (side view).

Defending against the horse (the
order given, 'Charge for horse
and draw your sword').

Defending against the horse (seen from the side). Note the foot bracing the butt of the pike.

Position for guard duty.

THE DRUMMER

Drums were used to relay orders to the soldiers on the battlefield and while marching. Drummers were expected to know 'how to beat all the several points of war'. Unfortunately the exact drum calls have not survived.

There were usually two drummers per company, who were paid 12d. a day, the same as a corporal. They were mature soldiers, boy drummers were only introduced in later centuries.

The drum measured about three feet high, with a diameter of two feet. The skin was parchment and enclosed both ends of the drum. A single string was stretched across the lower skin to produce a rattling effect, in some ways similar to the modern snare drum.

The drummers were used to take written messages to the opposing side, and while doing so to spy.

The drummer would always be blindfolded when led to the enemy's camp or position.

Junior ranks would always remove their hats and bow in the presence of a senior officer.

The messages would often be sent between men who had previously fought alongside each other in Europe during the Thirty Years' War. Now they fought each other.

If the drummer made it too obvious that he was spying he could expect rough treatment.

THE SERGEANT

The sergeant was a non-commissioned officer (NCO). He would have been dressed in a similar style to the ordinary foot soldier, wearing the regimental coat.

The main distinguishing feature for the sergeant, and also a badge of rank, was a short pole-arm called a halberd. Although mainly used for keeping soldiers in line and for measuring distances, the halberd was an effective weapon in skilful hands.

THE ENSIGN

The ensign was chosen from among the ranks of junior commissioned officers. His function was to carry, and protect with his life, the regimental colours.

The clothes of the ensign were always of good quality and often flamboyant.

The flag would often be waved extravagantly to taunt the enemy at the start of a battle. It was an extreme dishonour for a regiment to lose a colour in battle.

THE COLONEL

Each regiment was divided into companies. The company commanders, listed in descending seniority, were: the colonel, the lieutenant colonel, the sergeant major, and then a number of captains. The colonel, pictured here, was likely to be a gentleman. Officers of both sides wore expensive and fashionable clothes and, with the exception of the arms and armour, they differed very little from civilian clothes. A gorget worn around the neck was a sign of military rank. A coloured sash was also used to denote rank.

On the field of battle only senior officers used the partisan, a pole-arm measuring about eight feet in length.

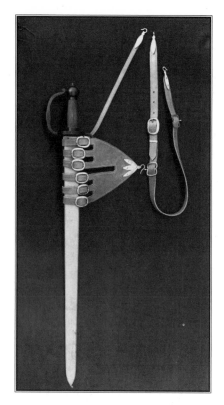

An officer's ornate sword belt.

A captain's leading staff. This is an exact replica of an example in the Tower Armouries collection.

THE CHAPLAIN

Each regiment of both sides of the conflict, theoretically, had its own chaplain. The protection and promulgation of their religion was one of the reasons given by both the Royalists and the Parliamentarians for fighting the war. During the early years of the war, chaplains recorded the proceedings of the armies to which they were attached. These accounts were subsequently used for publication in the press. The chaplains were, in effect, the very first war correspondents. The chaplain Simeon Ashe wrote about the Battle of Marston Moor. Oliver Cromwell employed Hugh Peters to give an account of the siege of Basing House.

The Parliamentarian clergy dressed in sombre, simple clothes.

If time and circumstance allowed, the chaplain would preach to the troops before a battle. The Parliamentarian army was renowned for the singing of psalms. Chaplains also seem to have been very active on the field of battle. At the Battle of Edgehill in 1642 it was recorded at the time by John Vicars that a number of 'eminently pious and learned pastors rode up and down the army through the thickest dangers, and in much personal hazard, most faithfully and courageously exhorting and encouraging the soldiers to fight valiantly and not to fly, but now, if ever, to stand to it and fight for their religion and laws' (*Cromwell's Army*, C.H. Firth. Methuen & Co., 1962).

Often working in terrible conditions, the surgeon would treat wounds with hot irons, and remove limbs without anaesthetic or antiseptic. The causes of infection were not understood until the nineteenth century.

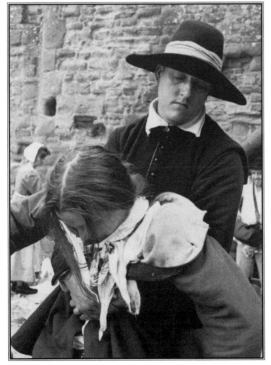

The chances of survival from a major wound were not good. Even a minor wound could turn septic, leading to blood poisoning or other complications, which would have been serious for a soldier already exhausted by fighting.

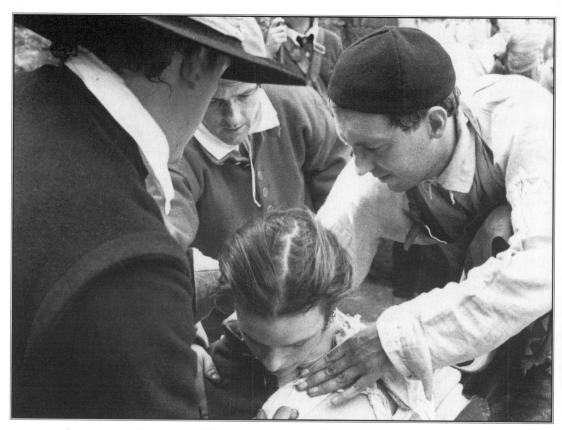

Some remarkable recoveries did occur. At the siege of Wardour Castle one Major William
Ludlow was hit in the stomach by a musket ball. It lodged near his spine having carried
with it a piece of the waistband of his breeches. The ball was removed and to quote an
account of the time '. . . he wonderfully recovered to be in some measure serviceable to the
publick'. Poor hygiene and only rudimentary medical attention led to more deaths from
typhus, known as 'camp fever', than from conflict.

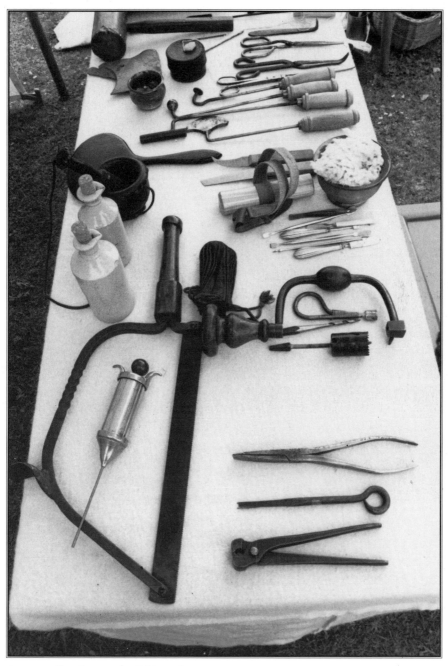

A range of implements available to the surgeon.

The ARTILLERY

A gunner with his assistants who were called matrosses.

A 'worm' used to remove debris from the barrel.

A sponge for cooling the barrel between each shot. If the gun became too hot the barrel could warp, causing it to explode.

A linstock, which was used to hold the burning matchcord to the touch-hole.

A saker, one of the larger field guns. Powder for the gun was usually kept in a barrel, but on occasion heavy paper or canvas was used to make the powder into cartridges. Cartridge paper is still used today, but for the more peaceful purpose of drawing. The larger guns took six to eight horses to pull them. Oxen were also frequently used for this purpose.

The gunpowder for the artillery had to be kept in a rain and sparkproof container. The animal skin on top of the box would have been used to cover the touch-hole in wet weather.

A Falconett. This cannon fired an iron shot weighing somewhere between 1¼ and 2 pounds. The rate of fire for all artillery pieces was about fifteen rounds per hour. Ideally, a couple of field pieces were attached to each regiment of foot, but this did not always happen in practice.

Dry vegetation was often used as a wadding for the cannons. When rammed firmly on top of the charge, the wadding had the effect of keeping the charge compressed for an efficient firing. If the charge was fired without wadding the powder would not have the full explosive force needed to propel the projectile or projectiles.

All field guns were mounted on two-wheeled carriages of oak and elm. Initially the King had fewer artillery pieces at his command. The Board of Ordinance based at the Tower of London was under the control of Parliament. However, most of the officers with the specialized knowledge went to the King's aid at the beginning of the war. Queen Henrietta Maria and other Royalist agents went to Holland and France to sell some of the King's possessions, and sent back a number of cannons.

The matchcord, held in the linstock, is applied to the touch-hole previously primed with gunpowder.

The priming powder ignites.

There was a short delay between the priming powder igniting and the main charge firing.

A minion barrel on a hoist called a 'gin'. When travelling long distances, some of the heavier guns were dismounted and carried on four-wheeled 'block carriages'.

The matchcord used by gunners and musketeers was made from rope and saltpetre (potassium nitrate).

The match was soaked in a solution of saltpetre and then left to dry in the sun. After baking in an oven the match was ready to use. Huge quantities of match were used by musketeers. A garrison of 1,500 men at Lyme used five hundredweight of match in twenty-four hours. During the siege of Devizes the occupying force ran low of match. The soldiers were ordered to search the houses and remove all the bedcords to make into match.

CAMPS AND GARRISONS

Soldiers' canvas tents.

An officer's tent.

A soldier's quarters in a garrison.

Stokesay Castle. This thirteenth-century fortified manor house was garrisoned for the King at the start of war. In the summer of 1645 it was seized by Parliamentarian forces after a siege. It remains largely as it was in the Civil War and is now owned by English Heritage.

Two soldiers on guard duty outside Stokesay Castle.

Soldiers had to turn their hand to other duties when in a camp or garrison.

Popular pastimes for periods of relative peace might include a game of dice (below), cards (right) or backgammon (p. 120, seen being played here by the ladies of a garrisoned house).

The playing of backgammon.

The taking of snuff was
fashionable among the gentry.

The playing of any game was forbidden on the Sabbath.

The food was basic but generally of good quality, offering a reasonably well-balanced diet.

Cooks, known as sutlers, supplied the food to the army. They were civilians attached to the baggage train. The food was cooked in cauldrons over an open fire.

When on campaign the food tended to be that which could be preserved most easily. Cheese and hard tack – a dry bread – formed the basis of the diet. It was supplemented with beef, bread, fish and mutton. On occasion the food supply broke down. The Earl of Essex's army spent six days with very few provisions, while marching to relieve the City of Gloucester.

Beer and, sometimes, cider were supplied to the soldiers.

The food would improve when the soldiers were garrisoned. The desertion rate was also lower.

Members of both armies were often billeted with civilians, sharing their food.

A stoneware bottle, often referred to as a bellarmine. This name came from the popular belief that the face that appeared on the side of the bottle was a representation of Cardinal Bellarmino (1542–1621), one of the leaders of the Counter Reformation. These bottles were copied in the seventeenth century from originals imported into England in the sixteenth century.

A range of seventeenth-century food, which was probably only available to officers while in a garrison.

Women did form part of the baggage train, but, unlike foreign campaigns, relatively few wives accompanied their husbands to war.

Soldiers' dependants and widows received nothing from the military, and unless they could find a niche in the baggage train they were very likely to become destitute.

The women 'camp followers' were largely English, with a few Scots, Irish or Welsh wives of soldiers. They were a cosmopolitan mixture of respectable family women, petty criminals and tradeswomen. When food was scarce it was likely to be the women that suffered first, soldiers had to be kept fit to fight.

Women who were unattached might possibly earn their food by laundering, sewing, cooking or practising basic medical aid.

Most wives were left at home. It might be many months without any news before families were re-united.

Leaguer ladies, whores, often attached themselves to a baggage train.

A barber and his assistant would have formed part of the baggage train.

Garrisons were vital both for the summer fighting, where they offered a defensible position, and the winter quartering of the troops. During the early part of the war, defence of a garrison was more likely to be successful than attack. One method of attacking a garrison would be to attempt to destroy the gates, always the weakest point of a building. A petard was often used for this purpose. The petard was basically a metal pot full of gunpowder which was attached to the gate. By necessity the fuse was short, and the men involved in planting the weapon were in danger of being caught in the blast, hence the saying 'Hoist by your own petard.'

Broughton Castle was garrisoned for Parliament by the owner Lord Saye and Sele and his two sons John and Nathaniel Fiennes.

Broughton was briefly captured by the Royalists in 1642.

This room in Broughton Castle was used for meetings between John Pym and other pre-war opponents of the King. The room has three external walls, and can only be entered by one door at the top of a narrow staircase. It made the ideal meeting place for people not wishing to be overheard.

Basing House was a large fortified palace belonging to the Marquis of Winchester. After several sieges it fell to Cromwell and the New Model Army in 1645. The bombardment lasted six days. One hundred Royalist soldiers were killed and twice that many captured. The house was razed and very little remains today, but massive earthworks and scattered atmospheric ruins give some idea of the huge scale of the original buildings.

The seventeenth-century octagonal dovecote at Basing House.

A first-hand account of a siege comes from the diaries of Richard Symonds, a soldier with the Royalist Oxford army: 'Thursday April 24 1645. Cromwell's Horse and Dragoons ruined some of our Horse that quartered about Islip of the Lord of Northampton's command. . . .

'. . . and this day they demanded the delivery up of Bletchingdon, a house belonging to Sir Thomas Coghill. . . .

'. . . wherein Colonel Windibanke had 200 foot, sans workes, and provisions only for two or three days.

'About two or three of the clock Friday morning the Colonel valiantly gave up the house and all his armes etc. beside 50 Horse that came thither for shelter . . .

'. . . and all this without a shot.

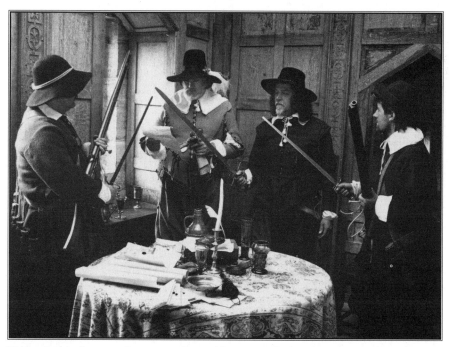

'Friday in the afternoon, he was condemned by a council of war to dye, and those that
were his councillors and advisors, viz., Leift-Colonel Hutchinson, Major Earnley, Mr
Eedes, were disabled for ever bearing armes any more.

'Satterday 3d of May. Colonel Windibanke was shotte to death, after he was reprieved from Wednesday before.' (Extract taken from Richard Symonds, *The Complete Military Diary* (ed. Stuart Peachy). Partizan Press.)

This book is dedicated to the forgotten soldiers of the King and of Parliament, who fought and died during 'This war without an enemy'.

USEFUL ADDRESSES

The Civil Wardrobe
Manufacturer of Practical Period Costume
Newtown Road
Newbury
Berks RG14 7ER
Tel. 0635 43806

English Civil War Society
Mary McDonald Watson
Thornton House
Bowbridge Hill
Gillingham
Dorset

Sealed Knot
Membership enquiries:
Mrs Margaret Smith
11 Ings Way
Ingbirchworth
Penistone
Sheffield
Yorkshire S30 6GL

For accurate copies of polearms, leatherwork, helmets, swords, matchlock muskets:

Two J's
32 Ashfield Drive
Anstey
Leicester LE7 7TA

New and secondhand books relating to the English Civil War and the seventeenth century:

Paul Meekins
34 Townsend Road
Tiddington
Stratford-upon-Avon
Warwickshire CV37 7DE
2 first-class stamps for catalogue

PLACES TO VISIT

Basing House, nr Basingstoke, Berks.
Opening times: Wednesdays to Sundays during summer months 2 p.m.–6 p.m.
Tel. (0256) 467294

Bickleigh Castle, Bickleigh, Tiverton, Devon
Royalist stronghold
Opening times: 2.00 p.m.–5.30 p.m. Please ring for days.
Tel. (0884) 855363

Broughton Castle, Banbury, Oxon
One of the best surviving examples of a fortified medieval mansion in
England. Broughton became a meeting place for leading opponents of the
King during the pre-war years. The castle was garrisoned for Parliament
during the war.
Opening times: May–September – Wednesday, Sunday and Bank Holiday
Mondays; July – Thursdays also; any day by special appointment.
Tel. (0295) 262624

The Commandery Civil War Centre, Worcester
Opening times: all year, Monday to Saturday 10.00 a.m.–5.00 p.m.;
Sunday 1.30 p.m.–5.30 p.m.
Tel. (0905) 355071

Leeds Castle, Maidstone, Kent
Site of a Parliamentarian arsenal during the Civil War and avoided the
normal fate of being slighted.
Opening times: mid-March–October, daily 11 a.m.–5 p.m.;
November–mid-March weekends 11 a.m.–4 p.m.
Tel. (0622) 765400

Littlecote, Berks.
Houses Royal Armouries Civil War arms and armour
Opening times: from April 10.30 a.m.–5.00 p.m.

Oakwell Hall, Nutter Lane, Birstall, Batley, W. Yorks.
Historic house near battlefield of Adwalton Moor 1643. Home of the Batt
family during Civil War.
Opening times: daily – telephone for latest details.
Tel. (0924) 474926

Pontefract Castle, Pontefract, W. Yorks.
Remains of the Royalist Castle besieged three times during the Civil
War – the last Royalist stronghold to fall in the north of England.
Opening times: daily, Monday to Friday 8.30 a.m.–7 p.m./dusk; weekends
10.30 a.m.–7 p.m./dusk.
Tel. (0977) 600208

The Tower of London
Opening times: all year, 9.00 a.m.–5.00 p.m.

Warrington Museum, Bold Street, Warrington, Cheshire
'Cromwell was Here!' Permanent display on Civil War in Warrington.
Opening times: Monday to Friday 10 a.m.–5.30 p.m.; Saturday
10 a.m.–5 p.m.; closed Sunday/bank holidays.
Tel. (0925) 444400

Photographic Notes

Equipment used in the production of this book:

Two Canon EOS 100 bodies
Two Canon EF 28–80 mm 1: 3.5–5.6 USM zoom lenses
One Canon EF 100–300 mm 1: 4.5–5.6 USM zoom lens
One Canon EF 85 mm 1: 1.8 USM
One Canon EF 50 mm 1: 1.8
One Canon Speedlite 430 EZ
Monopod with quick release head
Small Stepladder

Film used:

Kodak T MAX 400
Ilford HP5 PLUS
Ilford XP2

Technique:

Action shots all taken on shutter priority with an ideal speed of $1\frac{1}{2}$ times, or more, of the focal length of lens. The shutter speed was never allowed to become less than the focal length of the lens in use to prevent 'camera shake', except when 'panning' the shot where a slower shutter speed was used to blur the background and foreground (as in top photo on page 12).

Battle Scenes

Most of the battle scenes were taken standing on a small stepladder from behind the people watching the display. I always use a monopod to keep the camera steady. This combination allowed me to change my position quickly to follow the action as it moved up and down the field, as well as giving a better view of the battles.

The 100–300 mm lens was ideal for the battle scenes, using the 300 end to pick out individuals from the mêlé as in the lower photograph on page 18.

PORTRAITS

The re-enactors were very helpful and always willing to pose for photographs, but the best shots were nearly all candids.

A wide aperture helped to limit the depth of focus, eliminating distracting backgrounds.

Wide brimmed hats are very authentic, but they create deep shadows across the face. A flashgun to the side of the camera to give a small burst of 'fill-in' flash usually remedied this problem.

CREATING AN IMAGE

The picture of the cavalry troopers on page 24 was the result of a conversation with a re-enactor early in the day. The cavalry was due to come off the field immediately after the battle and travel a short distance along a country road. I saw this as a good chance to produce a photograph of tired soldiers as they would have been fighting for over two hours in heavy armour. I sacrificed watching the first half hour of the action so that I could make a recce of the gateway they were due to pass through. Making sure I did not get near the battlefield and keeping to the public highways I found my ideal spot. They would be coming uphill, passing within a few feet of me. There was a wonderful backdrop of unspoilt English countryside, much as it must have been in the seventeenth century, and without a powerline in sight. I worked out which lens I would need and probable shutter speed and aperture. The day was overcast with frequent rain so a 400 ISO film was essential to give a fast enough shutter speed to prevent camera shake blurring the image. In this case I used Kodak T MAX 400.

I took up my position at the gateway well before the cavalry was due to arrive to get ahead of the crowds. I had my camera mounted on a sturdy monopod and fitted with a 100–300 mm lens, using the one lens to take both the picture on page 24 at 300 mm, f8, 1/350th sec., and the lower portrait on page 27 at 100 mm f4.5 1/125th sec., with a small amount of fill-in flash.